Magic in Ancient Greece: The Hist
Practiced

By Markus Carabas & Charles River Editors

John William Waterhouse's painting, *Circe Offering the Cup to Odysseus*

About Charles River Editors

Charles River Editors is a boutique digital publishing company, specializing in bringing history back to life with educational and engaging books on a wide range of topics. Keep up to date with our new and free offerings with this 5 second sign up on our weekly mailing list, and visit Our Kindle Author Page to see other recently published Kindle titles.

We make these books for you and always want to know our readers' opinions, so we encourage you to leave reviews and look forward to publishing new and exciting titles each week.

Introduction

Magic in Ancient Greece

"Whether true or not, men had trusted in and believed these things." - Strabo

Magic today is the stuff of fairy tales and illusionists, something to titillate and perplex perhaps. But the prospect of "taking magic seriously" - despite the best efforts of occult movements in recent years, from the O.T.O. to the Chaos magicians in the 1980s - is still a very difficult pill for most people to swallow in the 21st century. This is not to say to disparage nor denigrate the efforts made by illusionists such as Penn & Teller or Derren Brown, who openly declare that what they do is to perform tricks, utilizing psychology and misdirection in order to entertain a willing crowd. These "magical practitioners" are artists well deserving of the name. In this case, taking magic seriously meant to actually believe in magic and take it at its word, outlined best in Owen Davies" summary of the anthropologist Max Weber's thoughts on the matter: "[Magic] promised to give humans control over a natural world governed by spirits."[1]

This view of Weber's could be (and has been) seen as some kind of definition of what "magic" is, or at least what it was to the ancient Greeks. Many scholars have tried and failed to isolate a clear definition of what "magic" is or was. Magic - as opposed to religion, personal or otherwise - is a notoriously difficult concept to pin down. In ancient Greece, "magic was not distinct from religion, rather an unwelcome, improper expression of it."[2] In other words, it's important not to think of it as a different definition of magic but to instead understand how the ancient Greeks believed certain aspects of magic functioned in their world. Since there are no surviving accounts of any full, contemporary hypothesis of what magic was, creating a picture of their belief in magic requires exploring what cultural factors shaped their beliefs. Often, the best surviving evidence of those beliefs comes from magic's biggest critics.

Most sources hail from the Archaic and Classical Periods of ancient Greece. It is in the Archaic Period that the ancient Greek culture, as people today know it, formed itself from the broken shards of the Mycenaean Palace Period scattered across the country after its collapse some 400 years earlier. Out of this formation came some early attempts at defining magic and magical practitioners as the liminal folk who were able to transgress the boundaries of the natural world in order to bring prized knowledge back to their mundane communities.

The Classical Period - which is probably the best known period of ancient Greek history - brought about the biggest cross-cultural event the ancient Greeks had ever witnessed: the Persian Wars. With this invasion from the East came a confluence of revolutionary ideas, a torrent of influences that would affect the Greek mind set for centuries to come. It was at this time that

---

[1] 2012
[2] ibid.

magical practices begin to be painted in hues of exoticism, the undertones of the unknown "other" that would influence the idea of magic and magical practitioners in Europe for millennia.

The Classical Period and the sources therein form most of the body of any book on the topic for a few reasons. The first reason is that it is from this period that a lot of surviving evidence originates. Secondly, it was during this time that the most interesting - and lasting - characteristics of magic ossified. Magic established itself in the ancient Greek psyche as a distinctly "foreign" practice, and, to some, it was a force that was dangerously powerful. Of course, what the ancient Greeks said about these "foreign" practitioners was in many respects a byproduct of their willingness to "Invent the Barbarian" by projecting their fears onto cultures they didn't understand.

In the same vein, it's worth analyzing the main critics of contemporary magic, namely the philosophers and medical practitioners of the time, since those individuals were not above "in-house" rivalries. The writings of philosophers like Plato indicate how magical terminology gained some of the pejorative connotations associated with it, and how those connotations were levied at rivals who, at least to the casual observer, appear to have conducted their business in a very similar way to their critics.

Magic in Ancient Greece: The History and Legacy of the Religious Rituals Practiced by the Greeks looks at the various people, places, and rituals performed over the centuries in ancient Greece. It offers a picture of an almost impossibly foggy aspect of ancient Greek scholarship. Along with pictures depicting important people, places, and events, you will learn about magic in Greece like never before.

Magic in Ancient Greece: The History and Legacy of the Religious Rituals Practiced by the Greeks

About Charles River Editors

Introduction

Free Books by Charles River Editors

Discounted Books by Charles River Editors

A Mage by Any Other Name

"The Greeks lived in the presence of "invisible" divinity," said the historian Levy-Bruhl.[3] This is a crucial idea, because despite what is known about ancient Greek philosophy, natural science and medicine, it's important to remember that, for the ancient Greeks, religion and magic were expressions of an obscure but deeply felt plane of existence they *knew* existed. Each apparently successful act of magic or religious ceremony was remembered fervently in the collective consciousness, while those that were unsuccessful were less readily and vividly remembered.[4]

To start, it's necessary to understand the terminology used to define who these magical practitioners were, and what acts they performed for the community. These are unruly and obstinate nomenclatures, which have been confused by the loss of sources, the prejudices of their critics, and the relentless eradication of time. However, by using modern lexicons in conjunction with literary criticism, these terms begin to paint a picture of general contemporary opinions and can be remarkably useful when looking at ancient source material.

It's also important to consider how the Greeks viewed the magical practitioners they considered to be "native" to their own land. Despite the fact that ancient Greece is considered by most to be a zenith of human and socio-cultural success in antiquity, the ancient Greeks were notoriously xenophobic even towards other city-states who spoke a similar language. Looking back at the legendary characters from the Archaic Period, and how they were viewed from the later Classical Period, will go a long way towards showing that the wider public opinion was not as damning as what scholars find in the surviving works of the philosophers and medical practitioners.

In order to conquer the beast, one often has to name it, at least in the realm of fiction. For that reason, we're going to begin our study of ancient Greek magic by studying the terminology used to describe magical practitioners (as well as those to whom the distinction "magical" would have been used in a pejorative sense) and to describe practices they were said to have employed. In the following chapter will begin to distinguish between Greek and non-Greek practitioners and the time periods in which they were said to have lived, as this has colored the way modern scholars view ancient Greek magic heavily. For the time being, however, establishing an understanding of what is meant by these terms provides a basis from which we can delve into the wider magical consciousness of Archaic and Classical Greece.

An exhaustive review of all the words that are related to magic throughout the Archaic and Classical Periods through to the Hellenistic Period would be extensive, but looking at the most commonly occurring "magical" vocabulary words can be nearly as illustrative. The key terminology consists of the words *agurtēs, magos, mantis, goes* and *pharmakon.*

---

[3] 1979
[4] Malinowski 1954

One of the most frequently found terms is *agurtēs* ("Beggar-Priests"), which seems to have been a common name for (and criticism of) certain magical and medical practitioners. However, looking at how Plato utilized the term sheds light on the working methods associated with the *agurtēs* and the services they offered: "Beggar-priests [agurtai] and prophets [manteis] go to the doors of the rich and persuade them that they have the power, acquired from the gods by sacrifices and incantations, to cure with pleasures and festivals any wrong done by the man himself or his ancestors, and that they will harm an enemy, a just man or an unjust man alike, for a small fee, if a man wishes it, since they persuade the gods, as they say, to serve them, by certain charms and bindings."[5]

Marie-Lan Nguyen's bust of Plato

---

[5] Plato *Republic* 364b-e

This is an interesting contemporary view of Greek religious practice. Greek religion functioned through the use of sacrifice and festivals. It was - as could be argued for many modern religions - a religion of propitiatory practice, because as many people know even today, no battle was begun, no legislature enacted, and no great undertaking was commenced without sacrificing to the gods first. This was not just a literary trope of the Homeric epic. As for festivals, the ancient Greek calendar was governed by the festivals it celebrated, either in honor of the gods or in honor of the fruits of human Endeavour, the success of which was deemed to have been the "will" of the gods.

Of course, if the *agurtēs* claimed to have received wisdom from this common religious practice of sacrifice and festivals, and they were able to make a living by offering the services this "reciprocal divine endowment" allegedly made them capable of, Plato's account suggests that he was most likely in the minority when it came to his lack of belief in the power of sacrifice and the possibility of discourse with the gods. Nonetheless, it's a topic addressed by Socrates (or at least in Plato's Socratic dialogues) and Aristotle.

A bust of Socrates

A bust of Aristotle

Furthermore, Plato's account is but one such criticism of magical practices. In fact, there is a recurrence of the distrust philosophers in particular had for magical practitioners. There was a common supposition that, if these supposedly gifted people were prepared to heal for money, then they must presumably be prepared to harm for that very same coin. This was a common complaint among the critics of magic in ancient Greece.

The term *magos* had widespread usage in ancient Greece, and its meanings varied greatly. It would not be a stretch to see that the etymology of the English word "magician" stems from the Greek "*magos*." Indeed, by the late 5th century, this word had developed many of the same characteristics in Greek as "magician" does today.[6] This is partly due to later surviving evidence, such as the plays of Sophocles (particularly *Oedipus the King*, discussed further below), Euripides, and Aristophanes, as well as the Hippocratic treatise *On the Sacred Disease*.

It is in these sources that readers can find *magos* become a negative, almost damning,

[6] Dickie 2001

nomenclature for a magical practitioner. Though often pejorative, its specific meanings could still vary wildly, from the likes of "enchanter" or "wizard" to, in the most extreme cases, "juggler" or "imposter."[7] The latter terms may not seem altogether too surprising, given the link between the meaning of *magos* and "magician," but the cultural significance of this word often brought with it a sense of charlatanry and deviousness, and it was used to that effect in the writings of philosophers and medical practitioners.

For example, writing in Ephesus in the late 6th century BCE, the philosopher Heraclitus took on this derogatory tone when speaking of the likes of the *magoi* (the plural of *magos*), due to their claims of being able to initiate people into "mystery cults." Even at this time the "mysteries" were beginning to be looked upon with scorn, as their secrecy created a vacuum into which suspicion would come from anybody who had not been initiated. What is noteworthy though is that Heraclitus does not yet use such words to imply that magic was anti-social in any way, a notion that was adopted by critics much later. These *magoi* were capable practitioners of an esoteric form of religion; keepers of the keys to that "unknowability of the Divine."[8]

[7] Sophocles *Oedipus the King* 387; Euripides *Orestes* 1497; Plato *Republic* 527E
[8] Sourvinou-Inwood 2000

Raphael's depiction of Heraclitus in *School of Athens*

An even darker version of the *magos* emerges in Hippocrates' *On the Sacred Disease*, written near the end of the 5th century BCE. Hippocrates wrote that the *magoi* claimed to be able to pervert the course of nature with their ability to control the weather and the sea. They even asserted they could pull the moon from the sky.[9] Conversely, Hippocrates believed that all diseases were caused naturally, the result of dispassionate machinations of the tangible world. This directly contradicted the *magoi,* who believed that they had the power to coerce the gods into healing those illnesses, which they caused based on their ineffable, divine whims. This is clearly an unabashed criticism from Hippocrates, who went on to use even more defamatory insinuations by accusing those magical practitioners of being impious, a very serious attack in ancient Greece, and one which could bring about the death penalty.

---

[9] 1. 29 – 30

A Roman image of Hippocrates

In Herodotus's *Histories,* however, the author - neither philosopher nor medical practitioner, but a noted "Xenophile" - was very interested in the religious practices of other cultures. Therefore, he approached magical practitioners from a different perspective to most of his Greek contemporaries. Less "sober" than most historical narratives today, Herodotus' *Histories* - written during the Classical Period (approximately 440 BCE) - regularly delved into the more esoteric (and often bizarre) aspects of contemporary cultures as he saw them. It is in this book that readers can find the continuation of the more positive earlier use of the word *magos* and its "foreign" associations. "Anyway, Deioces brought the Median race together into one nation and ruled them. This is the number of the tribes of the Medes: Bousai, Paretakenoi, Strouchates, Arizantoi, Boudioi and Magoi [i.e. Mages]."[10]

---

[10] Herodotus *Histories* 1.101

Herodotus used the word initially to mean anyone of the Median tribe, a people who lived in what would today be considered northwest Iran.[11] However, he elaborated by further distinguishing the *magos* as a "Priest or wise man" among the Medes, particularly one who interpreted dreams.[12] Nowhere in the *Histories* does the term *magos* hold the same negative connotations as it does in the works of the later philosophers, "doctors," or playwrights. One could infer from this that there were still those in the Classical period who saw the *magoi* as mystical wisemen who have access to a divine plane they could manipulate for good or evil.

Mantis is a word that often denotes a person of magical character, but like many of the other words attributed to magic, *mantis* also had its root in religion and continued to be used as long after the Archaic and Classical Periods. In Hesiod's *Theogony* (written sometime between the 8th and 7th centuries BCE) a *mantis* is described as "one who divines" as a "seer" or a "prophet."[13] This would have had religious rather than negative connotations at the time. Even in Homer's *Iliad* (also written in the Archaic Period) the *mantis* has the meaning of a "prophet" and needs the adjective "*kakon*" to denote any kind of definition as "Ill prophecy."[14]

A bust of Homer

It is in Thucydides' *History of the Peloponnesian War* (written sometime after the war, which

[11] 1.101
[12] 7.37
[13] 545
[14] 1. 106

lasted from 431-404 BCE) that *mantis* is first distinguished from the term *chresmologos,* which meant "giver or interpreter of oracles.[15] It is this depiction of *mantis* as "soothsayers" (compare that with later uses of the word *mantis* for "omen-mongers") that alludes to them having more of a magical rather than religious nature, though it was still not necessarily a pejorative term. The context in which this word is used suggests that these *manteis* were still held in relatively high regard in Thucydides' day, as they are noted as having a say in the decision to launch the military expedition to Sicily during the Peloponnesian War. Although in that passage Thucydides condemned them for the subsequent disaster, the fact that their practices were deemed legitimate enough to trust in the first place shows that, even towards the end of the 5th century, the use of magic was not deemed to be "folly."

Unlike *magos* or *mantis*, the term *Goes* does not have especially favorable definitions, at least for the most part. Herodotus mentions *goes* twice in *Histories*,[16] and although he doesn't really include a description of their practices, there is something of interest in these references. In both accounts Herodotus comments on a group of distinctly "foreign" people, of which he says, in an almost off-handed or dismissive way, that they are a "people of wizards." The interesting thing here is that the idea of wizardry is put onto people he considered as having a "barbaric" nature, meaning those who lived far away from the Greek mainland. This complies with the idea put forward by Edith Hall that the Greeks projected attributes regarded as bizarre and often undesirable onto alien peoples rather than simply documenting what they had found to be true from their interactions with them.[17] Whether Herodotus is projecting contemporary views of magic being something that is perceived as "bizarre" is not obvious in these passages, but it is noteworthy that he viewed "witchcraft" or "wizardry" as separate from "respectable" civic religion. Herodotus did not make any attempt to explicitly define wizardry or magic from religion, but it is interesting that he would credit all of their "barbaric" religious practices as being "wizardry." This could be seen as a negative view of magic in general if Herodotus wasn't a xenophile, but it's more likely that he simply distinguished the specific methods of magic from those of religion.

On the other hand, Plato distinguished *goes* from people who interpreted oracles by saying that they were the people who, while in a "frenzy," actually uttered the oracle given to them directly from the "divine." Despite the fact that Plato often criticized his rivals for dabbling in magic, this distinction suggests that Plato gives the *goes* specifically a lot more credit than is often thought. Plato believed that such "conversation" with the divine, or "receptions" of divine oracles, consisted of illusions unless they resulted in "receiving knowledge." Since the *goes* said that they utilized what they "heard" (aka "received knowledge") from the gods in their practices, this could be understood as being given a rather powerful meaning of authority by the philosopher, whether he said so explicitly or not.

---

[15] 8.1

[16] 2. 33; 4. 105

[17] 1989

The term *pharmakon* and its other relating forms (such as *pharmaka* and *pharmakis)* are the origins for the English words "pharmacy" and "pharmaceuticals," but the use of the words in ancient Greece is particularly interesting. These words appear in many sources across the ages, and it is necessary to be very selective. This is because *pharmakon* is especially widespread in literature and had an eclectic group of meanings, which often tended to be of a contrary nature. The more general meaning of "drug," for example, much like the English meaning for the word, held both positive and negative connotations, as it could be used for healing or poisoning.

Pharmakon appears in works as early as those of Homer and, in this context, thus had to be distinguished from its positive and negative effects with the use of an epithet. *Pharmakon* takes on the meaning of a "healing remedy" in the *Iliad*,[18] whereas, just like the term *mantis*, it needs an adjective to qualify it specifically as "evil drugs" (*kaka pharmaka*) in *The Odyssey*.[19] In *The Odyssey*, it also appears as an "incantation" and particularly a "philtre" (an intoxicating potion).[20]

The difference between these two meanings is based on the practitioner's intentions in the narrative. In the *Iliad*, Machaon is the son of Asclepius (the god of medicine), and he heals Menelaus's wound with a "balm." Machaon's benevolent use of *pharmakon* contrasted with that of the (generally considered "foreign") witch Circes, whose mischievous employment of "bewitching magic drugs" resulted in her turning Odysseus's men into animals in *The Odyssey*. As Dickie notes, although what Circe did was clearly wrong because it inhibited the freedom of good men, nowhere is there any real implication of her acts being impious or sacrilegious. The notion of impiety would come centuries later in Greek history.[21]

Liddell and Scott's lexicon of ancient Greek offers a number of meanings for the word *pharmakis*. The first defines *pharmakis* as a "poisoner, sorcerer, and a magician." The first example of such negative definitions comes from Hipponax, a writer of satires in the late 6th century, and an early example of the way negative connotations were being attached to words associated with magical practices and practitioners. Hipponax's use of the word *pharmakis* is not just a one off occurrence either, for it appears with the same meaning much later in the New Testament of the Septuagint, the Greek translation of the Holy Bible, demonstrating the long and unbroken tradition of magic in the ancient world.

According to Collins, however, another meaning for *pharmakis* is particularly interesting on a sociopolitical level. Liddell and Scott note *pharmaka* as also having the meaning of "one who is sacrificed or executed as an atonement or purification for others - a Scapegoat." It goes on to say that "since criminals and worthless scoundrels were reserved for this fate, *pharmaka* became a general name of reproach." This example shows just how a word, when affected by time and various contextual meanings, can evolve to have a definition far removed from the mostly

---

[18] 4.191
[19] 10.213
[20] 4.220
[21] 2001

benevolent connotation found earlier, such as in Homer's works. Aristophanes (Eq. 1405); Lysias (108.5); and Demosthenes (794.4) - all writing towards the end of the 5th century and the beginning of the 4th century - also record this use of the word *pharmaka*. By the time Horace and Lucan were writing in the 1st century BCE, the nature of *pharmaka* is something that is "fantastic and deadly to touch."[22] Thanks to this gradual transition, later down the line, the root word for *pharmaka* would be shared with the word *pharmassein*, which meant "witchcraft".

Time Confuses All Things

Magical practice - and particularly the opinion of that practice - depended very much upon the nature of the practitioner in ancient Greece and their critic. For that reason, it's important to consider how the "native" practitioners were considered, which requires looking all the way back to the Archaic Period (generally defined as being from the 8th century BCE to the early 5th century BCE). The surviving evidence from the Archaic Period generally shows that the Greeks of that age had a higher opinion of those who practiced magic.

Daniel Ogden, in his highly recommended source book *Magic, Witchcraft, and Ghosts in the Greek and Roman Worlds*, noted that the earliest "indigenous" magical practitioner was of that of a "shaman," the likes of which supposedly flourished during the Archaic Period.[23] Whether or not this supposition is actually true may never be known, but sources from the later Classical Period attest to them in such a way that historians infer this type of magical practitioner was at least well-established by that time.

These "shamans" were credited with the ability of detaching their souls from their bodies so as to make great "voyages of discovery." These voyages acted as a "mini-death" in some respects. The shaman would "cross-over" into another non-terrestrial plane and then return, in a form of "resurrection," more knowledgeable or powerful than they had been before.

Ogden defines the principal figures - and their supposed "flourishing" periods - in this "Shamanistic" group as the following:

Orpheus	(the "Mythical Era")
Trophonius	(the "Mythical Era")
Aristeas of Proconessus	(early 7th Century BCE)
Hermotimus of Clazomenae	(possibly the 7th Century BCE)
Epimenides of Cnossus or Phaestus (ca. 600 BCE)	

---

[22] Collins 2001
[23] (2002)

Pythagoras of Samos	(530s-520s BCE)
Abaris the Hyperborean	(possibly the 6th Century BCE)
Zalmoxis of the Thracian Getae	(possibly the 6th Century BCE)
Empedocles of Acragas	(ca. 485-435 BCE)

The scarcity of literary evidence from this period could be the reason for such a paucity of notable practitioners. Moreover, including Orpheus amongst a group of people associated with magic will not come as a surprise for most readers, but placing him in a fixed historical - rather than fictional - list may. The reason for this is that the Greeks, despite the lack of dependable evidence, would have most definitely considered Orpheus a "verifiably" historical character.

Another magical practitioner in this list may also raise an eyebrow on first glance: Pythagoras of Samos. Pythagoras became a legendary figure in his own day as a philosopher more than a mathematician, for which he is inarguably most famous today. [24] Predating both Socrates (ca. 470/469 - 399 BCE) and Plato (ca. 428/427 - 348/347 BCE), Pythagoras is credited for furthering and aggrandizing the "Pythagorean" philosophical methods, and his position in the canon of "great Greeks" was firmly established during that Classical Period. That said, by focusing on the sources that consider Pythagoras as a historical figure, rather than simply the progenitor of a philosophical method, it is possible to form a picture of him as a surprisingly "shamanistic" character.

---

[24] Burkert (1962)

A bust of Pythagoras

Fyoddor Bronnikov's painting depicting Pythagoras celebrating the sunrise

Pythagoras was born on the island of Samos, in the eastern Mediterranean, around 570 BCE. His location and timing of his birth are important because Pythagoras would have come to maturity just as the earliest "natural philosophers" were developing in nearby Miletus on the coast of Asia Minor.[25] This would come to influence his actions in southern Italy (or "Magna Graecia") later on in his life.

Pythagoras was said to have traveled extensively during his lifetime; most significantly, he was said to have traveled to Egypt, where he learned how to read the "language of the priest-magicians" ("hieroglyphics"). He also went "to the East," where he was said to have studied under the famed mystic Zoroaster himself (Zoroaster is discussed further below in the following chapter).

The Greeks long associated Egypt with ancient, arcane wisdom passed down through generations. Pythagoras himself was said to have been able to recall all of his past lives - an ability not particular to Pythagoras as a "shaman" but certainly credited to him with gusto by later authors - all the way back to his life as Euphorbas the Trojan, who was killed by Menelaus in Homer's *Iliad*. This spoke of his ability to transgress the boundaries of time and generation to access powerful lore from a "lost golden age". This was a common occurrence in ancient Greek thought. As most cultures often do, the ancient Greeks considered their earlier generations to have been somehow more "pure" or, at least, inherently closer to the divine. Therefore, to be able

---

[25] Kahn (2001)

to recall these times and the knowledge "lost" since then would have been considered a magical, if not divine, ability.

Pythagoras's learning of hieroglyphs would have been seen as such a particularly "magical" capability too. A compound word of the Greek words "Hieros" meaning "Holy/Sacred" and "Glyphē" meaning "Writing/Word," hieroglyphs were long considered to have magical qualities and were said to belong to the venerated Egyptian "priest-magicians." The understanding of this arcane, powerful language became another accepted truth about Pythagoras and was often referred to in the same context of his seemingly "superhuman" capacity for memory and learning. In fact, his later acolytes in Magna Graecia soon taught that there were three types of "thinking animals": Gods, Men and "Men like Pythagoras."[26] It was this knowledge, this learning of arcane and powerful, yet guarded, wisdom that his acolytes in Magna Graecia (where he settled and began to teach in the second half of the 6th Century BCE) soon appropriated into their own cult.

It's worth noting again that contemporary sources for this period are very rare, and as Zeller rightly pointed out, "the further away a document is from Pythagoras the fuller the account [of him] becomes."[27] However, though precious little is known from contemporary sources, what later accounts have to say about Pythagoras say a lot about the Greek perception of magic and magicians. After all, Plato developed his philosophy from Pythagoras, and though Plato also changed the conversation about him by emphasizing his more mathematical exploits, Pythagoras's more mystical reputation never fully went away in the Classical Period. That is, he was never fully "rationalized." Speaking in the 2nd century BCE - more than seven centuries after Pythagoras lived - Diogenes Laertius painted a picture of him that was entirely shamanistic: "He was in Egypt when Polycrates introduced him to Amasis by letter. He learned the language of the Egyptians, as Antiphon says in his book Men Excelling In Virtue, and he associated with Chaldeans and mages. And then in Crete he went down into the Idaean cave with Epimenedes, and in Egypt he also descended into crypts. He learned the secrets of the gods. Then he returned to Samos, and finding his homeland under tyranny of Polycrates, departed to Croton in Italy. There he laid down laws for the Greeks in Italy and he was held in high regard, along with his pupils. There were almost three hundred of them, and they governed the state in the best way, so that the constitution more or less was a true "aristocracy" [aristokrateia, literally "rule by the best"]."[28]

Here the account asserts that Pythagoras was associating with men of magic and even completing the one act attributed to all shaman-figures in ancient Greece: the descent into a cave. As mentioned before, this "cave" can be read as the "underworld" or a "spiritual death" that the shaman-figure must return from in order to gain his mystical knowledge. It was a transfigurative

---

[26] ibid.
[27] Zeller (1892)
[28] Diogenes Laertius 8.3

moment in the life of any "magician" and a defining moment in the career of a shaman. Diogenes places this episode right before the famous establishment of Pythagoras's colony at Croton, thus "laying down the laws" according to his learned wisdom.

This "law-making" episode in Pythagoras's life is not unique to him either. The legendary ruler of Sparta, "Lykurgos," was also said to have created laws after a visit to Egypt, laws that he made the people and kings of Sparta swear an oath to keep until he returned from his trip to the Oracle at Delphi. This was a trip, of course, from which he had no intention of ever returning. Both of these episodes were generally considered moments where Greeks (as those living in southern Italy at that time were considered) benefitted from contact with foreign wisdom, something to bear in mind when looking at the other side of this coin in the following chapter.

Pythagoras defines the "Shaman" character of Greek magical thought - the respected wise-man who dwelled on the fringes of our mundane reality and that of the "other" - but there were other magical practitioners who occupied a different place in Greek society, principally those who were considered sorcerers and mages. Based on surviving sources, Ogden notes that men were attributed with capacity to "manipulate souls, perform purifications, use incantations and manufacture binding spells.[29] However, there is another ability these "mages" were said to have mastered throughout the Archaic and even Classical Period: divination. Just like the Cunning Folk of Britain, the mages of ancient Greece were often attributed with the ability to divine or "see" the future.

Possibly the most famous of these "seers" was the blind prophet of Apollo, Tiresias. Tiresias's story is embedded in the greatest legends of ancient Greece. There are three accounts of his blindness. The first is that the gods blinded him simply for revealing their secrets, which was fairly insipid by Greek mythology standards. The second involves him becoming embroiled in an argument between Zeus and Hera over who enjoys sex the most, men or women. Tiresias had already spent seven years as a woman - the product of an earlier "punishment" doled out to him by Hera - so the celestial couple leaned on him for an objective answer. That answer came down on the side of Zeus, and Hera subsequently struck him blind for his impiety. The third unfortunate story of Tiresias's blinding has him stumble upon the goddess Athena bathing naked in a pool. Luckily for Tiresias, Athena is a little less quick to get angry than Artemis, who, when the hero Acataeon accidentally saw her in the same compromising position, set his own hunting dogs upon him, rendering him limb from lamentable limb. When Tiresias's mother, the nymph Chariclo, appealed to Athena for mercy, the goddess told her that she wasn't able to undo the curse - the curse of blindness seemed, even to the gods, a tricky one to make right again - but she would "clean out" his ears so that he could understand the language of the birds, and this would give him the gift of prophecy.

---

[29] Ogden (2002)

A depiction of Tiresias being turned into a woman by Hera

Whichever "origin" story one chose to accept for Tiresias's blindness, the fact that all three involve direct interaction with the divine gave added veracity to the character's prophetic ability. This veracity did not go unnoticed among the ancient Greek audiences of Sophocles" play *Oedipus Rex*, and this is particularly important when looking at Tiresias's treatment at the hand of that unfortunate monarch.

The tragic story of the king of Thebes, who, after he solved the riddle of the Sphinx, unwittingly murdered his father and married his mother, is possibly one of the best known in the canon of Greek myth. A moment often overlooked by the modern, rational eye is that of Oedipus's treatment of the most acclaimed seer in his kingdom. The king called upon Tiresias to help him find the cause of the plague, which was afflicting the city of Thebes. Given his past treatment at the hands of the gods, Tiresias was initially unwilling to reveal that it was the king's unfortunate actions that were causing the citizens of his city to suffer. Quick to anger, as most Greek heroes were, Oedipus soon became enraged at Tiresias, implying that he had no prophetic ability and was the pawn of his (in Oedipus's eyes) would-be successor to the throne, Creon. "[T]hat trusty Creon, who was my friend from the start, secretly stalks me and is eager to cast me out. For he has suborned this mage, a stitcher of devices, a deceitful beggar-priest, who can see only profit, but has a blind art. Come, tell me, how can you be a percipient diviner? How was it that your did not utter something to deliver these citizens when the song-stitching dog [i.e. the Sphinx] was here? Her riddle was not going to be solvable by just anyone, but true prophecy was required, It became all too clear that you had no prophetic knowledge either from the birds or from any of the gods. But I came along, ignorant Oedipus, and I stopped her. I hit home with pure intelligence, not with anything I learned from the birds."[30]

To a modern eye, it would seem that Oedipus was right in his dependence on his own rational faculties, rather than those supposedly bestowed by the gods, but to the contemporary audience this would have been an uncomfortable tirade. Initially, Oedipus bringing into question the accepted knowledge of Tiresias's divinely given prophetic abilities would have simply facilitated his unfortunately inevitable fall from grace. Oedipus's arrogance blinded him to his actions long before he struck out his own eyes.

But it's also possible that these specific insults would have struck a more lasting chord with Sophocles's audience since they would have been well known to them. Terms such as "deceitful beggar-priest [*agurtês*] who can see only (self) profit" were common to magical practitioners long before the first performance of the play (ca. 429 BCE). It's possible that Sophocles employed this language with the express purpose of unsettling his audience, using insults that they may have thrown at "mages" coming to their city and putting into question whether they had been right to do so or if, like Oedipus, their arrogance and flippancy towards a "vocal piece of the gods" might result in their own demise. The main tool of tragedy is, of course, instilling the fear of suffering the same fate.

Inventing The Barbarian

Despite the fact that it was easier to suspect that their own ancestors had access to magical abilities, ancient Greeks appear to have maintained a vein of sympathy for those abilities through to the Classical Period. The philosophers and medical practitioners were the principal and loudest voices criticizing magical practitioners in the Classical Period, but their opinion doesn't appear to have been that of the majority. There is material evidence of magical practice in the late Hellenistic Period, and there does not seem to be any evidence that this was any new phenomena, nor a resurgence of the ways of the Archaic Period. As long as the practitioners were Greek, their practices could very well appear to be "foreign" and they would still attract those in need. Conversely, when these "foreign" practices are projected onto non-Greek cultures, they took on the mantle of the malicious and the macabre.

When viewing magical practitioners not considered "Greek," the negativity expressed towards them and the practices they appeared to perform increased exponentially. In the Classical Period, Greeks tended to project any twisted religious or medical practices onto those they considered

---

[30] Sophocles *Oedipus Tyrannus* 380-403

"non-Greek." As Ogden pointed out, magic was not considered to be a "Greek" construct; it was inherently "foreign." This sentiment came to prominence in the Classical Period, which is unsurprising considering that it began with the most influential contact with cultures of the near East the ancient Greeks had ever experienced: the Persian Wars.

One of the best sources for the Persian Wars was Herodotus. A noted "Xenophile" and considered by many as "the Father of History," Herodotus's *Histories* was the first overtly "historical" account of major events in the Western literary tradition. These "major events" cover most of the 6th and 5th centuries BCE, effectively providing the cultural circumstances that led to the Persian Wars between the Greek city-states and the Achaemenid Empire of Persia. The invasion of the Greek city-states from the East brought with it new knowledge of the neighbors the Greeks never knew they had, knowledge that could be adopted, replicated and adapted for a new audience willing to pay for the manipulation of the natural order of things.

According to the Roman author Pliny the Elder, writing in the 1st century CE, the magical practices employed in Greece came from the teachings of Zoroaster, which were brought to Greece by the Persian *Magi* - specifically one named Osthanes - during the Persian invasion. Here again the name of Zoroaster is connected with magical knowledge and practice and, perhaps more pertinently, bringing in an untrustworthy aspect of religion to the Greeks. It's important to remember that these wars left a lasting impression on the Greeks' attitudes towards "non-Greeks," and not a positive one at that.

The Parthenon, the great jewel in the crown of the victorious Athenians, constructed in the wake of the Persian Wars, is laden with imagery depicting the victorious Greeks against their "foreign," unusual foes. The four sides of the Parthenon had metopes depicting these wars against "the other": between the Olympian Gods (Greeks) against the Giants (the "Other"); the Lapith people (Greeks) against the Centaurs (the "Other"); the Athenians against the Amazons (particularly "foreign" and "dangerous" since they were the quintessential antithesis of what was considered the "good Greek woman"), and the most blatant metaphor for the Persian Wars, that of the Greeks against the Trojans. This laden symbolism painted anything from the East, in particular, as malicious and untrustworthy. By the end of the Classical Period, the connection between magic and the East was firmly established, and not in a beneficial way for the practitioners.

Steve Swayne's picture of the Parthenon

These magical practitioners from the East held an odd dual role in the Classical Period of ancient Greece. Most of the sources that discuss them come from this period of outright antagonism. Sources from the 5th and 4th centuries BCE were generally hostile to anything from the East but particularly to their religion, which they considered to be nothing more than magical conjuring.[31] At the same time, however, this "practical religious knowledge" continued to have been sought out and utilized by local Greeks who felt like they were in need of their services, a need for more direct manipulation of the "unknowable". And as it turned out, the Greeks believed these "Eastern Mages" were capable of a number of different magical powers.

Necromancy was a somewhat troublesome area of expertise for the ancient Greeks. Many of their great heroes at some point participated in conjuring up a ghost or a departed spirit, including the hero Odysseus, but by the 5th century it was believed to be within the Magi's sphere of expertise, and that must have been a bitter pill to swallow for some.[32] In his tragedy The Persians from 472 BCE, written during the second Persian invasion by Darius the Great's son Xerxes, Aeschylus has Darius's widow (and Xerxes's mother) calling upon the spirit of her dead husband with the "Persian Elders" (whom Ogden presumes were mages) after she receives an ominous dream. The ghost goes on to confirm his widow's dream and predict the doomed

---

[31] Davies 2012
[32] Homer *Odyssey* 10.488-540, in which Odysseus consults the spirit of Tiresias.

expedition of their son, but the conjuring process, in itself, is interesting. "For this reason I have come here again before the house on foot, without chariot and without the luxury of former times, bringing propitiatory full libations to my son's father, things which soothe the dead, white milk, good to drink, from an unyoked cow, the secretion of the flower-processing bee, gleaming honey, offerings of water from a virgin spring, and an unmixed drink from its mother in the field, this restorative from an ancient vine. The fragrant fruit of the light olive tree, which always luxuriates in leaves, is here too, as are woven garlands of flowers, children of the earth that bears everything. But, my friends, sing hymns in support of these libations to the dead below, and call up the demon Darius, while I pour these honors to the gods below into thirsty earth."[33]

Offerings, hymns, obeisance to the gods and to the dead were all mainstays of Greek religious practices, so it's possible that Aeschylus either chose to imitate the religion he was familiar with in order to strike the right tone of legitimacy associated with them, or he was showing the similarities inherent between the two. It would have been exactly this kind of association, with their knowledge of religious practices being put to an "abominable" use, that would have struck an uncomfortable chord for Aeschylus's audience.

Interpreting dreams was another magical practice the Greeks were quite familiar with throughout their history. Herodotus tells the legendary story of how Cyrus the Great was prophesied to become king of the greatest empire the world had ever seen. Astyages was the last king of the Medes, the ruling class of northwestern Iran in the early 7th century BCE (or mid 6th Century BCE, depending on the source). He had a dream in which he saw his daughter, Mandane, "make so much water that she flooded his entire city, and the whole of Asia was flooded too." He told the mages about his dream, and their answer terrified him so much that, once she was of "marriageable age," he refused to give her to anybody he considered "more than below even a middle-ranking Mede." However, his fears were not abated by his second dream: "So Mandane took up married life with Cambyses. In the first year of the marriage Astyages saw another vision. He saw a vine grow from his daughter's genitals, and this vine covered all Asia, After seeing this he communicated it again to the dream-interpreters. He summoned his daughter, who was now with child, from the Persians. When she arrived he kept her under guard with the intention of killing the child she bore. For the dream-interpreters of the mages had interpreted the vision as indicating that his daughter's offspring would rule in his place."[34]

The child survived and grew up to become Cyrus the Great, the ruler of the Achaemenid Empire that invaded the Greek city-states during the Persian Wars. Here Herodotus is verifying the validity of the mages' ability of prophecy through dream interpretation, while simultaneously prophesying the invasion by a "Great Warrior" who would eventually devastate the Greek city-states.

---

[33] Aeschylus *Persians* 598-708
[34] Herodotus *Histories* 1.108

A discussion of magic as a projected version of "the barbaric" onto "the other" cannot be complete without the discussion of witches and witchcraft. As noted earlier, the Greeks had a very specific view of how a woman should act, and what was not part of the "Golden Mean" of female behavior in civilized society. Being as strong as men, being better archers than men, and generally "questioning" men (be that in household words or with battlefield tactics) was considered "bad form" by the ancient Greek patriarchy. The idea of a "foreign woman" would no doubt have filled them with dread and that could well be the reason for the stories surrounding the infamous witches Circe and Medea.

In Homer's *Odyssey*, Circe is called "of the many spells/drugs" (*polypharmakos*) when she met Odysseus and his men on her island, Aeaea. When Odysseus and his men arrived at her house, half of those sailors learned exactly how she acquired such an epithet. "She took them in and sat them down on chairs and thrones, and for them she mixed cheese, grain and pale honey with Pramnian wine. She blended baleful drugs into the food, so that they should forget their homeland completely. But when she had given it to them and they had drunk it down, she immediately struck them with her wand and shut them into pigsties. They had the heads, voices, bristles and bodies of pigs, but their minds remained unchanged and just as they were before."[35]

The leader of these poor sailors returned unscathed to the ship, and he told Odysseus and the rest what had happened. Odysseus, ever the rash hero, decided to go to confront the witch himself. On his way, however, the god Hermes met him and attempted to dissuade his approach. "My poor man, where are you going alone through the hills, in ignorance of the country? Your comrades are penned up like pigs in close sties in Circe's house. Do you come here to set them free? I tell you that you will not return, but remain there just like the others. But, come, I will free you from your difficulties and save you. Take this. Go to Circe's house with this good drug, which will keep the evil from your head. And I will tell you all the deadly tricks of Circe. She will make you a potage, and throw drugs into the good. But even so, she will not be able to bewitch you, for the good drug I will give you will prevent her from doing so."[36]

Here is a very early account of both uses of the word "drug". It was common for heroes to be aided by the divine, and Odysseus enjoyed more than his fair share of help. Circe, on the other hand, despite being credited as at least somewhat divine, employed the use of drugs to create a bizarre menagerie of conscious metamorphic beasts, seemingly just for her own amusement. The fact that she used her divine powers to attack these unfortunate men would have struck fear into any contemporary male Greek reader.

---

[35] Homer *Odyssey* 10.229
[36] Homer *Odyssey* 10.281

An ancient depiction of Circe and Odysseus

This depiction of Circe is also important due to its age. The Homeric epics came down through oral history, until they were transcribed sometime in the 7th century BCE. That means this is likely the first extant portrait of a witch in Greek literature.[37] Although the names later given to witches (*pharmakis* and *pharmakeutria*) are not mentioned in this passage, the term *"polypharmakos"* is explicit. Using drugs, balms, ointments and potions, Circe is able to perform a wide range of magical spells, from causing forgetfulness to transforming the men into animals and then back into humans again. Readers also later learn that she is capable of making herself invisible and is also an expert in necromancy, making her a true "Renaissance Woman" of the arcane.

The infamous Medea was, supposedly, Circe's niece, which would have afforded her an indirect link to divinity too. Although the fullest account of her exploits with Jason and his crew of Argonauts comes from Apollonius of Rhodes' *Argonautica* (written in the 3rd century BCE), her myth probably dates back as far as the 8th or 7th centuries BCE.

---

[37] Ogden 2002

An early 20th century depiction of Medea and Jason

The priestess of Hecate, the Greek goddess of magic and witchcraft, Medea helped Jason to find and claim the legendary Golden Fleece when he arrived at her homeland of Colchis in the Black Sea. Aside from confusing the skeleton warriors by throwing a rock into their midst, Medea helped Jason complete his other two nigh-impossible tasks with the use of magic, specifically *pharmaka*. She gave him an unguent to protect his body from the blazing breath of the fire-breathing oxen he had to use to plough a field, and she sedated the sleepless dragon with a potion while Jason captured the Fleece. She managed to help her lover one more time as they fled Colchis for Iolcus, though this method employed no magic: she distracted her pursuing father by killing and cutting up her brother and dropping him piece by piece overboard. Thus, her "introduction" to Greek myth already encapsulates her ability to employ her deadly art and ingenuity for good and evil.

Once in Iolcus, King Pelias refused to give up his throne - something he had agreed to do if Jason returned to him with the Golden Fleece - so Medea set about helping her new husband once again. When they arrived in Iolcus, Medea withdrew her father-in-law's blood, infused it with magical herbs and then replaced it, rejuvenating him in the process so that he could celebrate the return of his victorious son. The daughters of King Pelias saw this magical feat and implored Medea to help them do the same for their father, apparently naïve to the injustice their father had committed towards this powerful witch. In a play by Sophocles called *The Root Cutters*, of which only fragments now remain, we get a glimpse into the magical process Medea employed next.

"She covers her eyes with her hand and collects up the white clouded juice that drips from the cut [into the "evil plants" she has cropped] in bronze jars.

"The covered chests conceal cut roots, which this woman reaped, naked, with bronze sickles, while crying and howling.

"[Sophocles then records the incantation sung by the chorus of witches who helped her]

"Lord sun and holy fire, sword of Hecate of the roads, which she carries over Olympus as she attends and as she traverses the sacred crossroads of the land, crowned with oak and the woven coils of snakes, falling on her shoulders."[38]

Medea and her attendants performed this "plant magic" to make the daughters of Pelias mistake their father for a ram, which they subsequently slice into fine pieces and place in a pot while they believe they're performing the ritual that will rejuvenate him.

Ogden also notes that Medea and her witches would have commonly performed their rituals with their clothing "untied" - "the rationalization of this may have been that one performing binding magic should not herself be bound" - but Sophocles pushes the envelope of tragic symbolism again as he takes the notion to the extreme in making her appear not only "unbound" but naked.[39] Nakedness (outside of the "Heroic Nude" in art) was connected with wildness and barbarism in ancient Greece, and having Medea appear to "cry out and howl" while performing this abominable act would have added further dramatic aplomb to the scene. So awful, in fact, was this woman in the eyes of the ancient Greeks that Herodotus records that Medes changed their name so as not to be associated with her.[40]

---

[38] Sophocles *The Root Cutters (Rhizotomoi)* F534-6 TrGF
[39] Ogden 2002

Valid Grievances

By now it should be obvious that the number of remaining sources favorable towards magical practitioners is far outweighed by those that are unfavorable to them. The criticisms are legion, and though a lot of these critics are of a dubious nature due to having in-house motives for voicing their opinions, it is worth exploring those critiques further, especially concerning what the doctors and the law had to say about magic during the Archaic and Classical Periods.

In order to understand why philosophers and doctors felt such a need to attack magic and magical practitioners, it may help to isolate the underlying feature all three disciplines held in common. As Collins rightfully states, "in Plato and the Hippocratic author there is an emergent concern with magical agency and its relationship to divine forces."[41] Nature is of prime importance to all three genres of thought and practice; the earliest philosophical thought (which undoubtedly influenced everybody's favorite shaman, Pythagoras, in his youth) was centered on the forces of Nature, particularly the cosmos.[42] The earliest Greek scientists called themselves "Natural Philosophers" from the mid 6th century BCE.[43] Thus, being confronted by a group which claimed to be able to affect and dominate the "natural" way of the world, rather than simply observe and comment on it, would have had a jarring effect, to say the least.

Magicians from the 6th century onwards made all manner of wild claims as to their abilities. *Magoi* claimed to be able to pull the moon from the sky, change the weather, cause the sun to disappear, and have the ability to prolong life.[44] They claimed to be able to do such things by performing sacrifices and uttering incantations (*epoidai*). Although at face value this may not appear to be any different than contemporary mainstream religious sacrificing and prayer (aside from the more extravagant boasts), to the ancient philosopher these claims were considered too grand and far beyond what could be expected from the gods in return for sacrifices and incantations. Ultimately, the philosophers did not take kindly to the notion that the gods could, in some way, be bribed to do as the mage commanded.[45]

This idea leads one of the main sticking points of the criticisms of magic in ancient Greece. Philosophy and medicine in the Archaic and Classical Periods were not the sober, often secular fields of study they are in the modern world, because there was always a religious aspect to whatever observations were made by practitioners of both.[46] Philosophers such as Heraclitus and Parmenides, writing in the late 6th and early 5th centuries BCE, were extremely interested in the divine order of the cosmos, with Parmenides's work being steeped in mythological motifs, personifications and religious imagery.[47]

---

[40] Herodotus *Histories* 7.62
[41] 2001
[42] Warren 2007
[43] Kahn 2001
[44] Dickie 2001
[45] Dickie 2001
[46] ibid.

As time progressed, however, philosophers such as Socrates, Plato and Aristotle became less influenced by the writings of these early philosophers, and the study of philosophy came to be less dependent on religious imagery than Parmenides's work was. This is still not to say that it became entirely secular. Many philosophers were tried, and some were even severely punished by the law for being impious, with the most famous being Socrates, who was put to death for impiety and corruption of the young at the beginning of the 4th century BCE. That may have led to some of the more vicious attacks on those who claimed to be able to manipulate the gods through magical practices, simply because they went unpunished.

Ultimately, Plato was more annoyed by one magical practice in particular that he took as being deeply immoral: that of approaching rich men and "making promises of curing all their physical and social ills, for a price."[48] A defender of the magical practitioners could argue that Plato was simply vexed by the fact that he wanted philosophy to be afforded more respect in contemporary society than any dependence on the gods or on magical incantations or amulets. However, this would be too simplistic approach to how a contemporary of Plato would have seen magic and the potential damage it could have caused.

Collins points out that Athens had no official legislation against magic, and Plato perhaps believed this was a flaw he would rectify in his ideal Republic.[49] It does not appear, however, that magic in general is something that Plato disagreed with entirely and wished to have seen put to an end. Plato never said that he believed there was no such thing as magic; in fact, he wrote in his work *Theaetetus* that he approved of the use of *pharmaka* and even *epoidai* (incantations) to relieve pain in childbirth.[50] Instead, it is more likely that Plato simply believed that more stringent constraints should be put in place upon charlatans and magicians who sought to use their skills for personal gain.[51]

In fact, some attempt to impose such constraints may have taken place in the city-state of Teos in the early 5th century. The *Dirae Teiorum* (or "The Curses of the Teian State") is one of the only surviving records of any state having employed legislature to control magical activity, and each "law" takes on the form of a curse itself:

"1. If anyone makes harmful spells/poisons [pharmaka dêlêtêria] against the Teian state or against individuals of it, he is to die, himself and his family with him.

"2. In anyone obstructs the importation of corn into Teian territory by any means, be it by land or sea, or thrusts it back once it has been imported, he is to die, himself and his family with him.

---

[47] ibid.
[48] Plato *Republic*. 2.364b-c
[49] 2001
[50] 149c-d
[51] Collins 2001

"3. … [fragment does not survive]

"4. If anyone rebels against a Teian examiner or chief executive, he is to die, himself and his family with him.

"5. If anyone hereafter, being chief executive in Teos or in Teian territory … kills … betrays the city and territory of the Teians or the men on the island or in Teian waters or hereafter betrays the fort in Aroe or robs on the highway or harbors highway robbers or commits piracy or deliberately harbors pirates engaged in the plunder of Teian land or waters or deliberately conspires with Greeks or barbarians to damage the Teian state, he is to die, himself and his family with him.

"6. If anyone in office does not perform this curse at the statue of Dynamis when the games are convened at the Anthesteria or the festival of Heracles or that of Zeus, he is to be the object of the curse.

"7. If anyone breaks the inscription on which this curse has been written, or chips off the letters, or rubs them smooth, he is to die, himself and his family with him.

With that, the state was calling down a series of curses in defense of itself.[52] The first clause explicitly takes action to protect the city from harmful *pharmaka*. Given that the city was obviously not a physical but metaphorical body, Ogden also interprets this as including harmful "spells" in the definition of *pharmaka*. Most importantly, what is not in there is a condemnation of magic or *pharmaka* or *magoi* or any of the other magical terminology used by the Greeks in conversation at the time; the condemnation is on *harmful* magic alone.

Magical and medical practitioners occupied oddly similar places in ancient Greek society. Both promised to cure or prevent similar ills - often both using language that referred to, or invoked, the divine - and both often traveled to different cities offering their services (or "peddling their wares" depending on how one looks at it). The term "Beggar-Priest" (*agurtês*, which was one of the insults hurled at Tiresias by Oedipus) was often given to a traveling magician, but this was not a name given only to those claiming to have some control over the "magical." In fact, philosophers and medical practitioners often resorted to slinging it at their rivals in their own fields. Even Socrates was likened to one in Aristophanes's play *The Birds*, and the "father of medicine," Hippocrates, seemed to have taken the strongest dislike to this class of people.

Hippocrates lived during the Classical Period (ca. 460-370 BCE), and although it's difficult to know if the writings that remain were penned by him or not, one work called *On The Sacred Disease* is most often attributed to him. This treatise was the first to lay out Hippocrates's theory that diseases were not caused by the divine but were "natural" to the human condition. As it so happened, this idea of what caused illness was in stark contrast to what the magicians believed,

---

[52] Ogden 2002

which was that illness was caused by intermittent divine intervention. Medical practitioners, such as Hippocrates, on the other hand, believed that the magicians used "divine intervention" as an excuse for when their remedies had no benevolent effect.

In *On The Sacred Disease*, Hippocrates dedicated a rather long passage to calling out the ineptitudes and charlatanry of those he calls "mages" (*magoi*) and "beggar-priests" (*agurtēs*). "I think that the first people to have projected this disease [epilepsy] as "sacred" were men like those who are now mages and purifiers and beggar-priests and vagrant charlatans. These people purport to be extremely reverent of the gods and to know something more than the rest of us. They use the divine to hide behind and to cloak the fact that they have nothing to apply to the disease and bring relief. So that their ignorance should not become manifest, they promoted the belief that this disease was sacred."[53]

In that passage, Hippocrates employs the same language to describe those intent on curing a disease (i.e. a practitioner of magic with the same aim as Hippocrates) as the language used by Oedipus when speaking about Tiresias the seer. Daniel Ogden points out that *On The Sacred Disease* goes on to attribute "charlatanry, venality, amorality, compulsion over the gods, ghost aversion, incantation, drawing down the moon and astronomical control," among other outlandish methods, to the repertoire of those he deems "magical practitioners." However, as Ogden also notes, "to the casual observer, the author may not have seemed so different from the mages himself, and the dispute may well have seemed one internal to a trade. [Hippocrates] goes on, after this passage, to make dietary prescriptions of his own that strongly resemble those he abuses the mages for making."[54]

Furthermore, Plato echoes these methods in an attack on his own rivals. Could it be that the abstract, esoteric methods of most magical, medicinal and philosophical learning opened the practitioners up to the same kind of criticism? Possibly, but the actions of "mages" seemed to have been so bemusing, so alien, and so attractive that they developed an unsettling aura of being "foreign," which would ultimately come to define them.

Conclusion

To understand the name of a thing is to understand more than just how people refer to it. Names can change, and they can be adopted or replaced. In some instances, names can reveal more about the person doing the "naming" than the one actually being named. A very simple example comes from the 16th century, an era in which a comparatively small political and economical power at the time, England, had to compete with the magnates of trade and empire, Spain and France, in order to survive. Rather than engaging in open war with much more powerful adversaries, the small country took to employing individuals who had the skill and bravery to disrupt trade routes and profit from the acquisition of riches caught between the mine

---

[53] Hippocrates *On The Sacred Disease* 1.10-11
[54] Ogden 2002

and the market. These profiteers were royally sanctioned - if not quite celebrated - and, to some, they were seen as pioneers of freedom amidst the oppression of colonial powers. The operative term here, of course, is "to some" because, to others, namely the French and Spanish, these profiteers and pioneers were better known as pirates.

There is a lot in a name. One person's hero is another's villain. It is easy to assume from the sources that have survived the ages that rationalism took hold in the Classical Period and that the interest in, and employment of, magic dwindled at this time. However, that was not exactly the case. Put simply, wherever there was pain and suffering - both physical and emotional - or greed and a desire to control the natural world, there was an interest and a demand for magic and magical practitioners. Superstition has not left modern society, even in the 21st century, and it is important to remember what the historian Marcel Mauss said about the force of such collective superstitions: "It is public opinion that creates the magician and the influences he has."

Philosophers like Plato did, in fact, try to redirect the memory of such "shamanic" characters as Pythagoras to a certain extent, and to repaint him in a more rational light. With the luxury of tracing Pythagoras's legacy into the Classical Period and beyond, however, it's apparent that Plato's efforts were not entirely successful. While there was an audience for great, liminal folk heroes such as Pythagoras, Plato's hopes that he would be remembered solely for his mathematical and philosophical genius remained stymied. Audiences, after all, are the ones that govern the legacy of ideas, and the authors of the famous ancient tragedies utilized public opinion of magic and magicians to great effect. By tarring a true prophet with the same brush as those "beggar-priests" and "charlatans" the ancient Greeks met in their cities, the playwright cast doubts in the minds of his audience, doubts that could, as the events in the play warned, have deadly consequences. The ancient playwrights did not invent their characters but merely propagated myths that were integral to Greek society. Showing how a doomed figure like Oedipus failed to heed the prophetic visions of the respected seer Tiresias was no simple literary trope; it was designed to play upon the superstitions and fears of the contemporary Greek. Oedipus's fate, as a result of his arrogance and impiety towards the seer, was intended as a warning to all those who would listen not to dismiss lightly those who claimed to have access to the divine.

In the Classical Period, magic became entangled with propaganda. The Greeks had suffered hitherto unknown atrocities at the hands of those who were different from them, and this would have - as it does in all wars - solidified and confirmed old prejudices. The Greeks had interactions with foreigners for centuries before the Persian invasions, which created as much distrust as curiosity. When their distrust was finally confirmed, the Greeks began building an image of the "foreigner" that encapsulated all of their fears and all that was anathema to them. The same mix of curiosity, distrust and fear they had in magic – which was always considered a "foreign" concept - was now accentuated and hurled at any culture that was not Greek.

In Herodotus's work, however, readers see the other side of this coin, the reverence of a power to control the unknown, and the remnants of arcane and ancient knowledge that promised to reveal a plane of existence the contemporary Greeks were certain existed. Moreover, the Greeks believed they were at its mercy. Plant magic was an example of this "knowledge of the unknown". The ability to activate the dark powers that lay dormant in the flora that surrounded them would have excited the very darkest fears and reverence in the ancient Greeks. Being able to wield this power for good or evil was dangerous enough, but that power being in the hands of women - foreign women at that - would have inspired untold fear in the average Greek male. Sometimes, it provided enough fear to compel a city-state to enact laws.

The use of plant magic, and *pharmaka* in particular, encapsulates the duplicity of ancient Greek magic. The ancient Greeks were often quite fastidious in keeping records of legislature, which means that historians have quite a lot of literary and epigraphical evidence at their disposal. However, given that very little of that legislature - a force the ancient Greeks took very seriously and placed a lot of faith in - condemns magic in general is particularly revelatory. Like *pharmaka*, all magic had the capability of being employed for good or evil. The 5th century laws of Teos were not only written down during a period when some writers were trying to label all magic as foreign, they took on the form of curses themselves. Furthermore, these laws did not condemn the practice of magic but only the utilization of those powers with malicious intent towards the city as an entity.

In sum, the belief in magic persisted beyond the Classical Period, and the condemnation of its practitioners, though voiced in many arenas, was nowhere near a unanimous opinion held by all. The force of superstition would (and will) always be bolstered by the human need and desire for help and a good story. To the ancient Greeks, the heroes, demigods, and gods were not simply figments of their imagination, nor mere aspects of their religion, but verifiable characters in a very real history. Magic was simply a skill or ability that, although more prevalent in their past, was very likely handed down through generations of adepts. And, as Malinowski pointed out, every time a spell or ritual or *pharmakon* was seen to have worked, the reputation of magic and the magical practitioner was bolstered once again.

Online Resources

Other books about ancient history by Charles River Editors

Other books about Ancient Magic on Amazon

Bibliography

Burkert,W. 1962. "Goes. Zum griechischen Schamanismus." *RhM* 105: 35-55

Collins, D. 2001. *Magic in the Ancient Greek World* Blackwell

Davies, O. 2012. *Magic: A Very Short Introduction* Oxford

Dickie, M. 2001. *Magic and Magicians in the Greco-Roman World.* London

Hall, E. 1989. *Inventing the Barbarian* Oxford

Kahn, C. 2001 *Pythagoras and the Pythagoreans* Hackett

Levy-Bruhl, L. 1979. *How Natives Think* Michigan

Malinowski , B.1954. *Magic, Science and Religion: And Other Essays* New York

Mauss, M. 1972. *A General Theory of Magic* Routledge

Ogden, D. 2002. *Magic, Witchcraft, and Ghosts in the Greek and Roman Worlds* OUP

Sourvinou-Inwood, C. 2000 "What is Polis Religion." in R. Buxton (ed.), *Oxford Readings in Greek Religion* Oxford

Warren, J. 2007 *Presocratics* California

Zeller, E. 1892. *Die Philosophie der Greichen in ihrer geschictlichen Entwicklung* Reisland

Free Books by Charles River Editors

We have brand new titles available for free most days of the week. To see which of our titles are currently free, click on this link.

Discounted Books by Charles River Editors

We have titles at a discount price of just 99 cents everyday. To see which of our titles are currently 99 cents, click on this link.

Printed in the USA
CPSIA information can be obtained
at www.ICGtesting.com
LVHW022213130424
777362LV00008B/917